THE NIGHT MY GLASS SHATTERED

Miatta E. Dorley

Forte Publishing

First Published in 2018
Published by:

FORTE Publications
#12 Ashmun Street
Snapper Hill
Monrovia, Liberia
[+231] 777155-923
[+231] 881-106-177

FORTE Publishing
7202 Tavenner Lane
208 Alexandria
VA, 22306

FORTE Press
76 Sarasit Road
Ban Pong, 70110
Ratchaburi, Thailand
[+66] 85-824-4382

http://fortepublishing.wix.com/fppp
fortepublishing@gmaill.com

Printed in the United States of America
Copyright © 2018 MIATTA E. DORLEY
All rights reserved.

ISBN: 0648182320
ISBN-13: 978-0648182320

Dedications

This book is dedicated, with all of my love, to the memories of my son, Sgt. Maxwell Robert Dorley, and my Dad whom I lost three months after Max's death. You both are forever in my heart.

Acknowledgement

I wish to thank my Lord and Savior Jesus Christ for carrying me through my most challenging and difficult times.

To my dear friend and prayer partner Mrs. Joy Chineze Eromosele, for encouraging and pushing me to get this work done, thank you, I cherish your life and friendship. To Sonia Harshbeger, for loving me through my most difficult moments. Gabriel Amo, thank you.

To my dear aunt, Hawa Nancy Vincent, whom I call my sister, for her deep commitment and loyalty always, I love you very much Nana.

To my niece, Michelle Davidson, who inspired me to write this book.

To Helena Poweh and her children, lots of love. You prayed for me through my trials.

My Nephews John Dunbar, Emmanuel Bobby Gul and Lionel Paries, you guys are my true sons.

The Providence Police Department, especially Col. Hugh Clemens, I would not have made it without you guys. Thanks.

My Liberian communities, other Africans brothers and sisters you people are great. Many thanks.

My state of Rhode Island family, a people with a big heart, you are the best State in the whole country. Thanks.

To my transcribers, Madam Fatu Johnson, Mr. Peter T. Jomah and Winston, sincere thanks.

To my Grand Children, Amanda Mamala Dorley, Robert Maxwell Dorley, Jardin Patterson Cuffey, Jasmin Elizabeth Cuffey and My very best friend in the whole wide world, Isaac Gbehan Eliacin. I wouldn't have made it without your love, BBF- {Best friend forever]. To Prof. William Pellicio and Prof. Audrey Hugh of the Community College of Rhode Island.

To my large family, Rhode Island's finest men and women in *Blue,* Providence Police Department.

Lastly, to the Mayor Angel Tavers, Providence City Mayor during Max's death and to the State of Rhode Island.

Lastly, a debt of gratitude to the FORTE Publishing team for making my publishing dream a reality through this book.

A Special Appreciation
to the following of Rhode Island

Lincoln Chafee, former Governor
Senator Jack Reed
Senator Sheldon Whitehouse
Rep David Cicilline
Rep Jim Langevin

Personally, I am indebted to these men
for all their efforts to my family and me
during our dark days. The entire Liberian
community owes a debt of gratitude for their
endless sacrifices in pushing the DED case.

Steven M. Para,
Commissioner of Dept. of Public Safety

Contents

THE NIGHT MY GLASS SHATTERED

Introduction

This is the true story of a little boy that made a lasting and impactable legacy on an inner city.

It is a story of his journey from West Africa that took him and his family to the USA.

It might both astonish and, at the same time amaze one's heart, how could such a child go through all of this and yet remain focused up to the last moment he takes his last breath. But it is more of a miracle coupled with a resilient heart than magical.

I believe that there is something inside each one of us that has a portion of a beginning- the One that created life. It moves us in attaining His purpose in life. This also teaches me that life is not and should not be tied down to a temporary situation, especially a negative one. There is a line in a song that says," When one door is shut, another one is opened." You only need to believe and walk through it. And rightly, this little boy did just that.

But as the renowned play writer, William Shakespeare, and King Solomon of old said, ''life is but an empty dream''. I believe my little boy knew that too well, and he put his heart and mind to that dream. He lived and worked opening doors before others. He tried being all things to all he met. He was kind-hearted, generous and hopeful, owing from his tumulus and humble beginning.

I really do believe that death is an "awakening of a soul"- the opposite of what some people think. I am not saying that I am strange, just a bit different in my thought that there are those that think that when someone dies, all is over. But I personally believe that the passing of one's life, although physical, should not be emotional only because there is a life that exists through the legacy that is left behind. It is predicated upon this that I want to share with you those moments that formed his life. I would like that you join me in rather celebrating his life than mourning it.

This boy is Maxwell Robert Dorley-AKA Max or Bobby as his friends and family called him.

Prologue

April 18, 2012

The day was ordinary. The skies were bright and sunny, whilst the African heat burned my skin. Yet, I felt a sense of accomplishment because our little church in Vincent Town had just had its roof installed and we worshipped there for the very first time.

Emotionally, one could even say that I was on a spiritual high. To celebrate, I called the pastor from the church to go over plans for the donation I had made.

With my errands done, I went home around 6:30 pm, where I went straight for my bath, after which I decided to relax with a glass of Lemonade. About half way through my drink, the glass slipped from my hand and fell onto the floor. It was the night when my glass shattered.

A mother should never have to bury her child... this is against the natural order. What most people do not know is this never gets easier. One gets better at dealing with it, suppressing it and outwardly appearing calm. But there's not a living moment that it is forgotten.

A smile, a giggle, a kid here or there, a teenager struggling for attention, a sound or thought... anything can be a trigger- just anything. Then, your walls come crumbling down all over again. Many times, I wonder, why erect the walls in the first place? They never tend to last; they never do.

Memories flashed as I sat staring at Max's coffin, but for the most part, I just stared right through it until everything blurred. I could not believe that my child was laying there- cold, unmoving, gone! One thought kept coming to me over and over – "Parents are not supposed to bury their children, it should be the other way around. Children are rather the ones to bury their parents".

I guess I needed some rationality but none came. So there I was, forced with a harsh reality.

I watched as thousands upon thousands of sympathizers poured into the funeral parlor to offer their condolences. I also noticed that every state official and even some United States government officials were there to give their tributes.

Strangely, I found myself reflecting on how our time here is but fleeting as wild flowers, seasonal. My grief froze briefly and then I asked, "Did I do enough? Did Max do enough?" I used this unique perspective of Max's life to reflect on how many challenges a single parent has to go through to bring up a child and now look at how broken and frustrating life has become. All of my high expectations and dreams are dashed and in a matter of minutes, my whole life changed as though I were watching a movie. Only this time, I am the star of this movie.

The Night My Glass Shattered

This was my traumatic experience. What follows, is the true story of not just how I lost my son, but also how my life got shattered with that loss.

Different Place / New Strokes

Our life story begins in a small village in Liberia, West Africa. Vincent Town, named after my great grandfather, lies on the outskirts of Montserrado County, on the high way leading to Bomi Hills, in western Liberia.

Right before my birth, it seemed that I was doomed for failure. Both of my parents came from two different ethnic groups. My father was eighteen (18) years older than my mother was and had four other wives. Having many wives was a sign of wealth and power in our culture.

In addition to their marriage being arranged, mama explained that she was never in love with him. I was born a year into their marriage and problems had already begun. My mother moved back with her mother and father, where she stayed until she gave birth to me. My grandfather," Grandpa", as I called him, was a paramount chief of his Clan, the Gola tribe. In this type of environment, we were supposed to live as a high society family but it was not so at all.

My mother refused to go back to my father thus she was forced by conditions to continue living with her parents. As I got older, I realized that we were living on this compound of seven other huts in addition to ours, with grandpa's extended families. Although each wife had her own hut and children, at times, it seemed like a battlefield because each wife was always trying to compete for and conquer grandpa's affection.

My grandma, being the first wife or head wife as she was called, was always the one that had to sit back and quietly receive all of the insults, attacks, and mistreatments.

As a child, I am sure that all of us living with them at the time were aware of what was going on. Although we lived in different huts in the same compound, we got along fine and looked out for one another.

When I was about six years old, my grandpa informed all of his extended families that he was going to marry another wife, western style. As I grew up, I found out indeed he was married to my grandma and the rest of the wives, but their marriages were considered African traditional marriages and had little value in our society at the time. It has since changed over the years. It was during that time I also realized that my own father had abandoned me because other children made fun of and taunted me, I began to ask question about him but my mother would refuse to give me any answer. My mother had since remarried and had two other children. I lived with my grandparents until one day when my grandpa came and announced that he was taking me along with some of his younger children to live with his new wife.

Existing

When we arrived at our new home, I was astonished to see that grandpa had built a new two-storey home for his wife. It had a bathroom and kitchen inside. There was also a stove, a kerosene refrigerator and several nice furniture sets within the house. The home even had a power generator to give out electricity at night. Interestingly I noticed, they hired people to clean the house and to take care of the yard. Despite the newfound wealth, we-the other children not by the wife-hardly experienced the comforts around us. Our part of the compound had no running water. We had to use the pit latrine and bath facilities outside.

In addition to sleeping on a bare floor with just a piece of cover cloth, we, especially me, had to learn immediately the etiquette of our new home. Considering that not all of these were in grandma's place, my work was cut out of a hard place for me.

We had to, in the absence of the hired help, learn how to clean and flush the toilet although I'd never used it and was not allowed to use it. In my struggle, a funny thing happened. One day, I lost my footing and came tumbling down the stairs. I'd never seen them. I guess they scared me a little. It was a completely new experience.

In all this, I knew that one day, hope would come. In the meantime, my 'hope' came through the visits of my grandpa, albeit far and few in between, and my mother, Yeajua [Small Ma].

My grandpa came over one day and announced to us that he'd take two persons over to stay at his wife's relatives. One of my younger uncles, Amos, and I were the ones picked. We went to live with her parents- in-law in a small town in the northwestern part of Monrovia.

Life there was no better. In some ways, it was worse. On most days, they treated us no better than domestic helps. As one of the two girls in the home, I took turns with the cooking, cleaning and washing. At times, we even had to go to the nearby bushes to fetch fire wood- a normal chore of a village child especially in those days.

At the age of ten, they felt that a child was able to perform all of the household chores. At times, I had to help cut the grass in the yard in addition to fetching water from the creek. Life seemed so difficult; hardship and mistreatment, all seemed like a normal way of life. I didn't know any better on how children were meant to be treated.

Whenever Grandpa and my mother visited, which was twice a year, they brought some provisions for us.

While they were around, our foster parents allowed us to clean ourselves and put on clean, good-looking clothes. This was highly pretentious because as soon as they left, we went back to wearing rags. Mom and grandpa could bring sweets and other treats that made us feel happy, but whenever I tried to explain the living conditions to them, grandpa would say that having a difficult childhood was for my good. It would produce a well prepared adult out of me for the future, he'd say.

It was always a mixture of joy and sadness for me. Joy because of the sweets and treats they brought us; and sadness because of their failure to act upon my complaints. At times, I even felt as if they were equally responsible for our ill-treatment.

Our foster parents beat on us for almost everything we did. But while grandpa and mom were visiting, we were treated with decency. Punishments were left out or avoided by our foster parents.

The only escape I had was on the days our foster parents allowed us to attend school or church.

****

One good thing we had in our lives that was very beneficial was that, they always allowed us the chance to go to church on Sundays. The Sunday school teacher taught us how to pray and one of my favorite prayers has been, ''be anxious for nothing, but in everything by prayers and supplications with thanksgiving let your request be made known to God. And the peace of God, which surpasses all comprehension will guard your hearts and minds in Christ Jesus'' Philippians 4:6-7.

I put all my trust and depended upon God's will for my life. I was privileged to have one teacher who believed in me and always encouraged me to study hard and do my best. I must give God the praise that people around me never looked down on me. If anything happened to me that was sympathetic, they would reach out to me. I remembered at one time in my life, I just wanted to die. I could not go out to play with the other children because I had so many chores at home to do.

Coming from school one day, I overheard one of my neighbors say to a friend, how sorry she felt when I walked by. Life for me at that point in time seemed impossible. I was now at the age of fourteen.

Raping

One night while sleeping on the bare floor, I met an unfortunate fate. My foster mom's son entered the room where we slept. He crept towards me and literally picked me up. I was sleepy, but not asleep. I wondered what this was all about but I could say or do nothing. If he was strong enough to lift me... and in no time, we were in his room. He dropped me on his bed. My heart was at war in my chest. It felt like a tsunami had hit me right in my belly, ripping my chest apart. I was certain that everyone in the house could hear the frantic pounding of the blood-pumping organ. It pumped more than blood this night. It gushed out fear. Raw, uncut fear. Even the bed vibrated beneath me.

He wasted no time in ripping off his clothes and mine. By the time he was done, I had no illusion what was coming. That was sad. I knew something was afoot. I knew it wasn't good. I just didn't know what it was nor how to stop it. I feared angering the grandfather. I feared being made a liar. I feared for what this unknown would do to me.

Like an animal, he jumped on the bed right on top of me, knocking the wind out of me. As I gasped for air, he tussled between my legs. Fumbling with him and making a way to enter me. My little frame and my resolve were no match for the overbearing beast over me. I had never seen a fiercer animal; never seen my foster brother so singularly purposed as this. I had no experience with this behavior. My fear ran deeper than just a victim's did. He personified it.

One would think that after such savage behavior, there'd be remorse of some sort; not in the least. He had rolled over on the bed at the side of a trembling me, which he noticed not. He carried a smirk and smiled victoriously a few times. He had won himself a trophy. One he intended to keep.

Truly, from that night, he felt he was entitled to my body. He believed he owned me, at least I thought so from the way he went about taking me, possessing me, objectifying my body and even the way he comfortably removed me from the scene as he had his way with me. I was but an object to satisfy his desires and nothing more. Though little, it was impossible to miss his utter disregard and disrespect to my person.

In all this, I felt so used and dirty that I would take a bath whenever I had the chance. I even reached to the point where I washed my body with disinfectant as a way to cleanse me from not just his filth but the immorality and abomination. I hated him! I detested him so much and even wished him dead. It took me many years to forgive him and move on with my life.

In retrospect, I have forgiven him but I fully appreciate those that feel such acts are not worthy of forgiveness. He violated more than my body; he raped my tender soul. How does one absolve oneself from such? How does one even forgive the culprit? How does one begin to pick the pieces up after such shattering reality?

None of those questions has easy answers. I had no guide to navigate those troubled waters. It was a dark period. Had it not been for my Sunday School teacher, Ms. Clara, I doubt I would have survived. She found a way to get under my skin; a way to gain my trust enough so that I was able to tell her. More importantly, she listened. No judgement, no sneering, no blaming; she just listened at first, and then she gave me the encouragement I needed to go from one Sunday to the next. Each week I survived my torture because I knew on Sunday, she would be there.

Every Sunday, I looked forward to getting fresh encouragement in the Lord. The teacher talked about how much Jesus loves and cares. She told me to read John 3:16, ''for God so love the world that he gave his only begotten son that whosoever believes in him shall not perished, but have everlasting life''.

That one verse in the Bible altered the course of my life. I made up my mind that living here with my foster parents was only temporary and that grandpa would not believe whatever I told him. I felt that my existence depended only on running away.

I wish I could say it was bearable. No it wasn't. I just waddled through it. At times, I recalled the love of Christ. This was something she had drummed into me. For some reason, it seemed to have worked.

I also knew that I needed to get to a safe environment. With my mind was made up, I sought my opportunity. My chance soon came in January of 1969 right after I turned fifteen. One night when the moon was high and shining brightly, I woke. I made sure everyone had gone to bed, then I opened the back door with few of my clothes tied in a bundle, and slipped out into the night. I snuck out and never looked back.

The Escape

I must have walked all night long. Whenever I heard a vehicle approaching from either directions, I would lie down flat on the ground. I could not afford to be caught by my foster family, whom I hope had not discovered my absence yet. I risked being kidnapped by *heartmen* for ritualistic sacrifice, as this was the common practice in those days. I just walked.

Anywhere away from that house was better. I had no food, water, nor money; I was not about to let that stop me. After a while, I realized I had gone far. I could hear the sound of strange animals. At times, as I approached some areas, animals ran away in fear of the sound I made. These encounters frightened me.

They forced upon me the realization that I was in eminent danger. Every time there was a shaking in the bush, I hurried along as quietly as possible. I walked with unusual speed all night long until I reached the next town in the twilight of that morning. I was so exhausted to have even thought about being caught.

God has a way of keeping us safe. It is not always clear nor is it easily understood, but it exists. As the psalmist notes in Psalm 23:4-5. Even in my child like faith, I knew God was going to take care of me.

I didn't wait to get oriented, once I found the station, I hailed a taxicab and told the driver that I had no money to pay the fare but he could kindly take me to Bomi Hills Motor Park, my destination, my grandpa would pay him.

Surprisingly, it was that easy. The taxi driver got me into Monrovia and then to the Bomi Hills Motor Park. Additionally, he put me into another car headed for Bomi Hills. He paid the driver the fare and asked him to collect both fares from my grandpa upon arrival. You see, grandpa was well known nationally.

He was both a judge and a paramount chief. This was a bit relieving, at least to me right now. The taxicab arrived at my grandpa's and dropped me off at my destination. He explained my situation and they summoned grandpa who came immediately. He paid the fares for the rides. He was judging cases in his court so he didn't stay long.

Grandpa sent across the street for Aunty Miatta, the one whom I was named after, and she took me over to her place until that evening when the whole family gathered for discussion. At the family meeting, the conclusion was that I move and live with my grandma.

That night, I could not sleep despite my best efforts. I was still in disbelief. I'd woken this morning in hell but here I was, in the relative comfort of my grandparents compound surrounded by family. This thought alone made me feel safe. I wept bitterly for as long as I could. The mosquitoes that evaded my new quarters stole any sleep that would have come. It would be a completely different kind of battle I'd be fighting at night.

****

Pregnancy

I soon realized that there were lots of natural food. There were cold-water fish fresh from the creek, avocados, guavas, mangoes, coconuts, palm nuts, oranges, etc. Our main diet was rice, cassava products, and palm oil. I ate like a malnourished teen. The truth is, I was underfed. Seeing all this food only fueled my appetite.

Nothing seemed odd to my family nor me. At times, I'd feel sick but I passed it on to something I may have eaten or overeating. The more I ate, the larger I grew, almost in proportion. This too seemed normal to me. It, however, was hard to shake off the heaviness lodged in my belly sometimes. No amount of eating accounted for it. My body was changing way too fast for my 'discomfort'. However, I was just glad I only had to battle mosquitoes at night. That was livable.

After living there for about a month, the old folks, experienced in many matters, gave me the news that changed my life forever. I was no longer innocent, nor was I a child. I found out that I was pregnant. The concept was not totally lost on me. How the heck did that happen? Here was how I learned that a consequence of sex was unwanted pregnancy. Sadly, in my case, it was repeated rape. How could I carry a child? I was myself a child.

I recalled how my stomach 'fell'; dropped deeper into my belly when I heard the words. Into that spiral, dropped my hope, aspirations and dreams of ever getting an education and fending for myself a better life.

I had seen what having babies did to girls my age. Most were not even in school then here I was, having tasted western education, now having to lose it all because some buffoon decided my young body was his personal fiefdom to rip and do horrible things with. How was that even fair to start with? My soul was slipping into an abyss and I felt powerless to grasp it. With this, I was as good as dead. A life of a housewife was my best choice it seemed.

Stillbirth

My difficulties only increased. One, with knowledge came the added burden. I kept worrying. Then the physical wear on my barely matured frame. I ate like a hog. This served mostly to be a problem much later because; the child grew healthy and big.

During the entire pregnancy, I received limited prenatal care. We were at a distance from the limited number of health professionals. Moreover, my unique condition left me almost untouchable. I gave birth few months later to a boy. The baby lived for about six weeks and then died. All of this happened in 1969.

After a few weeks, I partially recovered from all the trauma from all the things I went through. I talked about getting back into school with grandma and she decided that I should go up to Mining Town to live with my aunt and her family.

At times before we can reach into the place that God has for us, there are many derails along our path.

My pregnancy was an easy one. When I was about seven months into my pregnancy, I went to the river to do some laundry. That night after getting home and doing my household chores, I noticed that the palm of my right hand had begun to swell up and was very painful. I could not sleep at all. By the next morning, the news had spread into my neighborhood and my home was flooded by my friends and other concerned neighbors. Some suggested that my aunt go to see the witch doctor as was the common belief and practice at the time especially in my tribe.

However, some experienced women advised my aunt to send me to the hospital for checkup. Although I was in pain and dizzy, I was worried about the distance and the harsh conditions that awaited me on the way to and from the hospital.

My aunt sent me to the hospital in spite of my travelling fears. I had to go because I was thinking much more about my unborn child than myself. I did not want anything going wrong with my health that would affect the fetus. I got to the hospital and an X-ray was done but the doctors could not find any cause of the hand hurting and swelling.

My grandma heard about what was happening to me and she sent for me in Bomi Hills, where I was given a very small room with only a small bed in it and that was it. I even wondered when I give birth where the baby would lay. My swollen hand was attended to with herbs from the bush until I felt better. During the rest of my pregnancy, I lived in Bomi Hills under those conditions until I gave birth to Max.

Before I gave birth, I experienced pains for about a week. I told grandma about it and on June 20, 1970 at about 10: PM, I gave birth to Max with the help of grandma and a traditional midwife in my small room. I was exhausted after giving birth; I went right to sleep with my baby by my side while grandma slept on the floor. One time during the night, a thief entered my tiny room and stole all of the little things and clothes that my baby and I had. By the time I realized what had happened and called out to grandma for help, whoever took our things was already gone. It was amazing and unbelievable to note that as destitute as I thought I was, someone as heartless as could be would steal from me and my baby. This taught me a lesson that at least I was good enough to be stolen from.

He was a cute baby and I loved him and there again I had to worry about his welfare. I thought he went through all those tough times during the nine months I carried him inside me, as his final major challenge. But there again he is stepping into even harder life conditions – after he had been born. The pang of fear I felt for my baby was a nagging ache, but again I reflected on that bible verse mentioned at the onset, and all of the goodness, the God of love continues to do for me and I believed that for sure tough times don't last, but tough people do.

New Place/Old Strokes

Re-existing

I arrived at aunt's house in Mano River on a Saturday afternoon. Mano River is a small Iron Ore Mining town, some fifty miles north of Bomi Hills. The road was rough and bumpy with thick tropical rain forest on either side. The ride was long and tough but we made it.

Although the Mining Company provided housing for their employees, I later realized that there were three different types of housing within the community. There were housing for the senior staffers - these had all of the amenities that any home in America could have. The lawns were well manicured; the streets paved and were occupied by mostly whites and a few African senior staff. Then there was a second batch of houses. Although the homes had electricity and indoor plumbing, they had less amenities. Those were for junior staffers- mostly Africans stayed in them. If any westerner resided there, they probably were all bachelors.

Lastly, there were housing facilities for laborers. My aunt's family lived in one of these units. The living conditions were cramped and no better than in our village. The only difference there was that, the buildings were made up of cement bricks. No indoor toilet, plumbing nor kitchen. An opened area structured with tight spaces, without any kind of privacy was used for cooking. Bath facilities were four rooms - two for the women and the other two for the men. You just had to wait for your turn if the rooms were occupied. One had to walk for about three minutes to get there.

Everything there was for "second class humans" if there is any such thing - the school, shopping center and even the hospital. Everything here was just substandard. Not much care was given to those intended to dwell in them. Segregation was a normal human way of life.

I met Max's father there. He was working in the housing development office as an eighteen-year-old Clerk. We started dating and in October of that year, I got pregnant. At least here, I had access to a health facility, although getting there was a bit difficult. I had to walk for about three and –a half miles back and forth. Mano River Company had built a hospital for its employees and their families. The commonest means of getting there was by walking or by getting a ride from someone.

I had to walk on unpaved roads with thick forest on both sides under pouring rain or 90'-105' degrees of heat. Human traffic was so heavy with people travelling back and forth to the mines. At the same time thick brown dust and gravel would hit me whenever a vehicle passed by, this was the only way I could receive prenatal care. Occasionally while in route to the hospital, I saw animals like squirrels, antelopes, monkeys, and chimpanzee. As for the chimpanzees, they often stood for a few minutes looking at us, crossing or running along the road. One time, on my way for treatment at the hospital, I saw a boa constrictor slowly crawling across the narrow gravel road.

The doctors at the hospital were mostly westerners. There were also African interns and their bedside manner was very good. The typical Liberian nurses had poor human relation skills. They were fond of making derogatory remarks like, "You foolish little girl you should have been washing your Mom's dishes, but here you are coming to have a baby. But wait until the day of delivery, you will feel it".

They scared obstetric (OB) patients, especially teenaged patients like me. Lawd knows I could do without this pressure. They didn't understand my situation nor what I had been through, they simply judged me and the rest of the other teen mothers in their care. It was a conservative system we lived in, but that was no excuse. This worried me a lot during the pregnancy. It brought the thought of abortion to surface. At this age, it would be premature and even dishonest not to state that the thought surfaced. However, I was certain that I never wanted it each time it did. Aborting this pregnancy was not an option. It seemed like the baby inside me was destined for something special. That perception just overwhelmed me. I would worry and cry but then I'll remove that fear and assure myself that nothing will happen to me as long as there is a good God, whose image I carried in my womb.

Mano River community was a small mining town. People had come from all over Liberia and the neighboring Sierra Leone [western boarder of Mano River] for employment. So everyone knew pretty much all of each other's affairs. At the hospital, there were girls that were around my own age group, some older women with their husbands, or spouses had tagged along for their doctor's visit.

****

Bitter Sweet

After delivery, food was very scarce. Some days all I would eat was a pack of coconut biscuits and a can of chocolate milk. This cost me about thirty-five cents and that was for breakfast and lunch put together. By evening, whatever grandma found, would be our dinner.

Again, I never got any postnatal care. My nutrition was so poor that my breasts could not produce sufficient milk for my baby. I had to supplement breast milk with water, boiled corn and stuff it down his throat. Imagine a baby just a few weeks old going through that. All of this took a toll on his health but it seemed he had to live anyhow because he was destined for a purpose.

The pregnancy of Max was such a tumultuous period in my life. It was as if someone above had opened a box of bad luck right over my life. Remember how I mentioned that the day after I gave birth our things were stolen? Well, what followed was pale in comparison.

My aunt's husband asked us to move out of the house in which we were living. In some families, the husband is a dominant force and whatever he says, happens. His wife could dare not challenge his authority. My aunt was devastated but there was authority over sympathy.

With no other foreseeable option, I took Max and sat beside the house until one of my beloved cousins asked her friend Gboyah to allow Max and I to stay at their place for a little while.

At that time, in those parts, phones were not available. The fastest means of communication was the telegram, which sometimes took weeks or even a month before people could get a message across.

Finally, a message got across and Max's father came down from Mano River to visit us. His stay was short but quite relieving. At least I didn't feel all alone as I'd been feeling for a long time. However, the joy of Max dad's visit was short lived. For I got news that when he got back to Mano River, he was fired from his job. Just as quickly as it came, it went. I could not understand why all these things were happening. My faith was yet young. I was opening my eyes to the world and I did not like what I saw.

Way too much was happening way too fast for my young mind to process.

We never saw or heard from him again until 1981, the time that Max travelled to the USA. We thought that Max's father must have attributed his dismissal to a bad omen because he visited us. What was I to think? He just stopped communicating. Not one single word. I was too hurt to be angry. If I meant nothing to him, what about his son? Did he deserve that treatment? What loving father does that? Questions flooded my mind. Sadly, I had no answers.

It was only after many years when he told us that after he was fired from his job, he felt broken and helpless as a man and father. He could not bring himself to face his fatherly responsibilities or us.

Living for Once

Punches to Peaches

My mother later got word of our situation and came down from Gbarnga, Bong County in the north. She took Max and I to live with her and my stepdad.

Living with them was less challenging, I had my own bedroom and food was plentiful. I couldn't recall the last time I had had good food, in ample quantities. This must be what heaven felt like. It could not be life. I could not have been living; for ever since I had known life, she was one mean sucker punching champion. She took no pains to swing; and swinging is all she'd been doing to me. This had to be heaven. Imagine I had enough food in my system that my breasts began pumping milk in excess of what Max could eat; trust me, eat he could. We even had other food to supplement the breast milk. This made me safer and happier. Life was finally good to us.

I felt that this was the beginning of the emancipation from the life of hardship and hunger for us and indeed, it was.

In the midst of all of this, Max was just an extraordinary child. He was a bouncy baby with a huge appetite. People were so drawn to him that whenever we went out, they asked to pick him up. I guess every young mother thinks that her child is special. Somehow, my instincts for Max ran deeper than this. I simply knew he was destined for great things. As young as I was, I promised to prepare him for this great task of his although I had no idea what it was.

Despite my optimism, little baby Max was not this magical child. In fact he was sickly. He suffered regularly from asthma. His attacks were so severe that we had to hospitalize him some times. On one of such occasions during his stay in the hospital, the first lady of the Republic of Liberia, Mrs. Tubman paid an official visit in the area, and she visited the children's ward of the hospital, she came over, picked up Max, and held him for a while. I supposed it does not seem like much seeing she's human and all, but to a struggling, depressed mother like me, just the fact that it happened was sufficient confirmation that my past would not define Max nor me. This was encouraging, pretty and unique. Max stayed in the hospital for about a week and we went back to my mother's home.

Over time, Max got bigger and stronger. I decided that I should further my education to improve the quality of our lives. By that time, I was still in a very low grade level and could not even be counted amongst the semi educated people, and so I could not get a job.

Mothers everywhere are always looking out for their children's welfare. I say this because even at my tender age I began looking for opportunities that would firstly improve Max's life, then mine.

Peaches to Pies

At this time, a friend's mother, Musucour gave me a cash gift of fifteen dollars. It was more than some would make in a month. Such generosities didn't happen to me, at least not in the existence I had been waddling through. This had to be a good omen. I took that money and started a business. I sold peanuts, coconuts, milk, candies and kanyan (a mixtures of ground cassava, peanuts and sugar all pounded together to make a cake), that gave me some extra cash to buy stuff for my baby.

When Max was about eight months old, and just started taking few steps, I could finally feel my freedom. Life seemed to for once, have stopped swinging. If things continued this way, I could still have a chance at my dreams. This thought pushed me on regardless of what I faced.

One day shortly thereafter, my mother told me one day that we had to move to Vincent Town to be with my grandma.

We arrived in my hometown, Vincent Town around mid-January 1971. The weather was very hot, the road very dusty, and the ride was long and rough. Occasionally the baby will make a wheezing sound. Obviously, he was tired from travelling for such a long distance. We had traveled for about six to seven hours.

Grandma was waiting for us with a steamy cooked meal of potato greens [the leaves of the potato tubal cooked more like collard greens]. It was choked with dried fish, fresh deer meat and red palm oil. It came with the ruby rich red indigenous Liberian strain of the delicious country rice. This was a traditional welcoming meal for someone loved and honored. Max and I were treated like guess of honor on that day. We had our meal after taking a cool bath and we settled in. Max ate well, as he was now learning to eat solid food. Grandma showed me where our room was. It had a full sized bed that was made out of straw and palm fond for mattress, a pillow, a plain white blanket, and a small table with a standing mirror.

My room was quite neat and cozy; I loved it! Grandma talked with us for about two hours after dinner and we all went to bed. I must have fallen right off to sleep when grandma left and my head touched the pillow. I was awakened to the sound of Max crying around 4: am because he was wet and hungry. I changed and fed him and he went back to sleep.

New Life

Vincent Town 1971

People in my village are up very early in the morning because most of them are farmers and Muslims who have to attend morning prayers. Grandma was no exception. But on that morning, she went a little late because she had to show me how things are done in the home and village.

Vincent Town is a tropical village with a lots of mango, avocado, a few orange trees and many other tropical fruits – as well as palm and coconut trees. It also had sugar canes. We had a banana orchard right behind the opened hut that was used as a kitchen. There were other exotic plants throughout the village. Grandma had a small backyard garden with vegetables for cooking; she also had some chickens, a pair of goats, a pair of sheep and other domestic animals. Our drinking creek was about quarter of a mile away from the town.

The Scornful A

There were many young girls of my age or a little older. They were all (somewhat) married or engaged to be married. Girls got married at a very young age. At first they and their spouses looked at me a little strangely, most of the men did not want me to befriend their wives, whilst the parents of the single girls did not allow them to come around me. I guess they did not want their daughters having children out of wedlock like me. All of this made me feel down and like an outcast.

I must admit, this level of self-righteousness nearly broke me. Contrary to the immoral notion of 'country' girls, I was finding out that in my village, morality was a religious thing. At first when I learned I was coming back to my home village, I thought it would be a joyous stay where my childhood

Miatta E. Dorley

friends would happily have me back and we'd play and enjoy life together; but it turned out differently.

Although I was a mother at this tender age, I still had childhood characteristics. I wanted to do the moonlight dances and plays like any other child in a rural settlement. I did not want this motherhood to rob me of my childhood fun and activities. Nor did I want to be defined only by it. I, however, knew that some girls wanted to play with me but could not do so because of the restrictions placed on them, I understood their situations.

Although I was rejected and avoided, baby Max on the other hand, enjoyed the benefits of being pampered by everyone in the village.

Because of my responsibilities, I had little time to roam and play with these girls. Instead, I spent quality time with baby Max. And this had a profound impact on our mother-child relationship.

An early memory of ours stands out often when I think of our relationship. When Max was about the age two, I got ill with malaria. It knocked me down so badly, I had to take to the bed. Worried about him all the time, I was somewhat consoled that he was being looked after properly. He would run out and play with friends and then come back frequently touching my forehead to make sure that I was okay. I don't know how much he knew or understood but his actions deeply moved me. I wish I had asked him this before losing him. It is often said that, nearest is dearest.

However, in the face of all this I remained prayerful and respectful especially to the elders of the village. This was incumbent upon me for several reasons. One, my upbringing. Two, the social status of my grandpa. Any behavior that was considered uncultured by any of his family members, was tantamount to his inability to rule his clan. We all knew that very well and dared not cross the red line. The rest was just natural.

The Joyful E

The overall view of my village was just beautiful. It was breathtaking. A.M.E Zion Church had just built their elementary and junior high school right upon the hill across the motor road from my home. I was elated because that was an opportunity for me to enroll in school at the beginning of that school year. This became my singular, most important goal.

There was no electricity; people used kerosene lamps to light up their homes or waited on the full moon to enjoy the light. Often, the night was assaulted by a fresh cool breeze. The older men would sit around to talk village politics. The older women would sit and tell folk tales and riddles to the children; while the young adults would play hide and seek.

It was common to hear the owls hooting; the bush goats crying out their "woo, woo" sound, the crickets making their whistling sound, and especially, the frogs with their "ribit, ribit".

After the harvest season, around November and December, at twilight, one could see wild plants and grass blanketed with dew, which made it to look like a sprinkle of snow.

The clan was gay in part because of the plentiful food and palm wine. We have two major seasons in Liberia: Rainy season and Dry season. We experience heavy down pours of rain during that period and the dry season is when the rice farms are harvested.

Occasionally, I would go fishing with the village women and that was exciting to me. Maxwell was a happy baby, he ate whatever I would give him, including the fish I would catch from the streams. Because we were now living in the village, I changed his diet to dry plantain and powdered milk. If I did not have enough money to buy his food supplies, I would put water in his feeding bottle. He would drink the water and just throw the bottle on the floor from our little bed.

Max was popular with the town folks. By that time my girlfriends and their parents were not afraid anymore to come my way. The young girls would pick him up, bathe him and have his hair braided because he had long hair. He was now the town's baby.

I grew to love living in Vincent Town, the wetness of the flowers due to the night dew gives the place a different feel. The men will sit under the Palava huts drinking palm wine and discussing the events of their day, anticipating their next course of action. Most of the town was surrounded with trees that gave the village a breezy and shady protection from the hot Africans sun.

After about two years, Hawa, my younger aunty, came to live with us. She shared the same room with Max and me. We bonded almost immediately. We even shared clothes, shoes everything except under clothes. This gave Max a second mom. We both took terms caring for him, although we treated him like a doll, by this I mean, we used to dress him up, carry him on our backs, braided his hair and all. We took him everywhere we went. My grandma, along with the other grand aunties in the village, took care of Max during the day while we girls went to school. The school authorities knew about the baby but did not ask or talk about it. Then, our communities were very conservative. Because I had gotten a child, I was not allowed in school. Several schools had 'policies' for that kind of frowned upon behavior.

There was a lot of fun in school, but not for me. I spent all of my free time with Max, thus missing out on most of those activities. My grandma instilled in me that it was my responsibility. Despite that, I was able to hang out with other girls from different villages, as time permitted. I befriended most of them over time.

Soon, the fun ended and I was about to graduate. I now had a problem as our school only stopped at junior high. During that time, I met one of my father's younger uncles. I explained the situation and he took me to another of

my father's brothers whom he believed
could help me.

Grandma My Rock

Grandma had always shown me
unconditional love. I often felt dejected,
alone in this big world but never around
her. She exuded nothing but love for
me. She never judged, never scorned she
just loved but did not spoil me. She
knew when to be firm and when to step
in and help me. She simply made it
possible for me to go through my
pregnancy. I pay this little tribute to her
but I could write an entire book about
her. Her endless sacrifices awed me.
Many times, she gave me her last food
or kept the best part of the meal for me,
knowing I needed the nutrients. Other
times, she bathed me, babied me and
then most importantly, gave me insights
of life. She made me strong, boosted my
confidence and made me feel invincible.
There was nothing I couldn't do or be in
her sight. This lesson stuck. In many
ways, I believe that in my darkest hours,
I survived because of her.

I loved her wise sayings. She'd say
something like, "My child, we all have
a chance of making our lives better.
Never allow one mistake to ruin it. See
it as a minor setback before reaching
your destiny."

I'd often just listen and nod or say,
"Yes Grandma."

"Look into the mirror carefully and
think what you want your future to be."

"Yes Granma." From that point on,
I started to think more positively. My
outlook was more enthusiastic.

She also reminded me, "As the first
girl child, a lot of people were looking
up to you and no condition was
permanent. You should take any
opportunity. If your uncle wants to
help, then you should accept his offer."

She went a step further and spoke to
my mother and stepdad about it. They
agreed to take care of Max until I
finished school on condition that I
would come during the weekends and
help them out.

But there was a problem: who would
I stay with, in the city?

City Life

Young Adulthood

One of mama's cousins, Victoria, that lived in the city agreed to host me, thus settling that problem.

When I agreed to move in with my uncle's family, it was on the conditions that I would help with their children and house chores. I was apprehensive yet I accepted and was grateful. It turned out that decision changed my life. , and my new journey into adulthood began. Both my uncle and stepdad got new jobs with the concession company, Bong Mines. Life only got better and easier for us. As I look back, it seems I always had help from above.

School was about two miles away from home and I had to be in school by 8:00 am. I was up as early as 5:50am. I cleaned up the house, took a bath and then walked to school. I loved home and school but I was now faced with an old demon, hunger. There was never enough food. Almost on a daily basis, I starved. Here I was in the fancy city with all its attraction, but hungry. The pinging in my stomach often brought me back to reality... I needed food. The insecurities of old resurfaced. I could not enjoy some of these wonderful things I was seeing simply because my basic instinct to eat, was barely being met. Coming from a place with plentiful to this sudden drought was somewhat hard to put in perspective.

I often reminded myself that I needed this education and other philosophical nonsense. If I may say, the truth remained: I was too hungry to do most of what I needed to do. I believed all right but I needed the energy to reach the goals. Food was more than a means to that end. It was life in itself. I knew I had to find a way around the problem.

I made some friends within my neighborhood, and at their homes, I ate most of the time. If you have ever been hungry for more than a few hours, you'd understand how profound this situation was... I was living in the midst of plenty but having nothing. At home, there was just not enough. The little we had could barely feed us. I had to eat around to get the extra I needed to live.

With that nailed down, the city was much fun. I got to go to the movies, beaches, parties, and other social activities with my friends on Saturdays, we also went out to the restaurant where I ate hot dog for the first time.

Hot Dog

Here is a serious situation I once faced. I had grown to love the fancy restaurants. I would stop and watch people go in and out of there. I'd smell their delicious food and get hungry all over again. My girlfriends knew that and, as a treat one time, promised to take me there. Beforehand, my girlfriend told me, "Miatta, we will go to this fancy place I know and we are going to eat some hot dogs and order some drinks. We'd sit there for as long as you like."

"Hot dog?" I thought. "Are you crazy or something? Hot dog!" This girl must have a plan to kill me." I had not yet processed this when she knocked me out of it.

"What do you think?"

"Well, I would love to go to this place, but there ain't no way, I am going to eat any dog. I don't eat dog meat. Frankly, I am a bit surprised to hear that girls liked them. In fact that people here could eat dog meat. Aren't dogs man's best friend? So why in the world would anyone be heartless to eat them?" I ended my sermon a bit harshly.

The looks on their faces were priceless. They all laughed out their guts. I might have sounded so silly and primitive.

Anyway, she told me between gasps and nearly hiccupping that; "Miatta, this is NOT actual dog!" she indulged in another round of laughter before saying, "It is just called that. But it is nowhere near dog, I swear. We won't break your 'law'." That gained her another round of deep, heartfelt laughter from the crew. There seemed to be a joke here and I somehow was the one making it. I sensed that now.

Soon, they brought the promised hot dog. At first, I was still skeptical. I cautiously opened it, tunred it over like a million times. I even smelt it a time or few. Then I took a bite. The saltiness of the pork sausage, mixed with the frest leaves and tomato catchup was unlike any I had had. My taste buds took no time in registering their pleasure.

I was unawares and would even not be bothered by the fact that every pair of eyes on my table was attentively watching my every move. They must have felt the buds accept those powerful sensations, as much as I did because they not only burst out laughing, they cheered. It truly was more than an understatement to say I'd enjoy it. I loved the thing. Those were some of the happiest moments of my life.

Life in the city was challenging otherwise. Between those sweet memories was the hustle of life itself. As a result, I had to enroll at one of the boarding schools on the outskirt of the city. I attended the Lott Carey Mission, a Baptist run institution for four years and graduated from high school there.

A few weeks after graduation, I went up and brought Maxwell and my younger sister, Zinnah to live with me on Gurley Street, Central Monrovia. We were again faced with another challenge, overcrowding conditions. This forced us to move to Duala in the Western Suburb of Monrovia with Mr. Steward, a gentleman that I was dating at the time.

Maxwell lived with me and attended the St. Mary's Catholic High School in Duala. He got adjusted and made a lots of friends within the community. I started a small business, selling retailed goods and provisions.

As I sit and reflect on our life's journey, I count on the many blessings and people that came into our pathway of life. Even as a child I gained so much strength and comfort from Maxwell. I discovered through many of life's lessons, that even as parents we learn so much from our children as we nurture them.

Some Peace

Baby Max No More

"I can't do it, not with her. we are never going to speak again."

"And who tells you I want to be friends with you? I don't even wish to speak to you again."

"Listen, both of you need to fix this. It will not be easy but you can do it. Now let's sit down and talk."

Maxwell was one of those children that was mature beyond his age. One could say he was an old soul in a young body. Maxwell hated confrontations, was never a mischievous child. He was somewhat a mediator that was always settling issues when there were problems amongst his peers. To him, life had a purpose. The inner purpose of life was for him to pursue and set goals and standards. Even as a child he would always let one know what he wanted out of life.

Interestingly, he always seemed to know what he wanted to be. If you asked him, "Max, what do you want to be?"

He'd say, "I will be a doctor, a fireman, or a policeman." These were always top on his career list, even during playtime he would play one of those professions. He was career conscious and always having his friends over for dinner. He was just full of life and laughter.

Travelling Shoes

I travelled to the States in 1979 but was unable to be separated from my son for a long period. I cried day and night, I couldn't eat nor sleep. I therefore had to come back home.

My uncle, Seh Vincent, had come to Liberia from America to get his two children, and his sister Hawa. They were to leave on 23 July 1981. On 21 July when Maxwell turned eleven years old he approached me on that evening and asked, "Mama, could I travel along with uncle Seh and the others?"

"What? They leave in two days. Many things need to come in place before anyone can travel. I'm afraid we may not have enough time. It would take a miracle or something."

"Yes Mama, then let's pray for one."

And that was exactly what happened. It began like this: I went to Uncle Seh and asked, "Could you be foster parents to Maxwell?"

He said, "Why don't you call and ask Sandra?" she was American. I did and she agreed and so that settled the matter. We now had to expedite the visa process.

The Vincents knew that America is a land of opportunities and that Maxwell would not miss out when he got there. We prayed and asked God, our heavenly father for the favor of obtaining his visa.

Maxwell's encounter with God was two days before he was to travel to the

United States of America. I told my son if he believe God, then God would answer his visa prayer. He answered with such a confidence like never before. We then prayed to get a visa expeditiously, and we went to bed.

To some, the process of obtaining a visa was frightening to say the least. They'd not even consider the prospect. For others, it is intimidating as well.

The next morning I set on my way to the American embassy. I arrived there at about 10:45 am on July 21, 1981. I was called in at about 11am, when the Consular interviewed and asked me if Maxwell was really my son, and if I could produce his birth certificate, he would grant me the visa. As I stated earlier, divine timing and divine favor works out just right for anyone who puts his/her trust in God.

Everything was just alright for me. I had a phone in my home so I called my sister Hawa and told her where to find Maxwell's birth certificate, charter a Taxi

Cab and come right up to the American embassy. She arrived about 11:40am before lunchtime, and we were blessed in obtaining the visa on July 22, 1981. I went right away got his plane ticket and did a little shopping for Max and gave some money to my uncle Seh for his wife Sandra to do some shopping for clothing.

Maxwell, uncle Seh, and aunty Hawa left Liberia for the U.S.A on 23 July that year.

Maxwell in US

Maxwell lived with uncle Seh, Sandra, and son Wilbert (Mr. Lee) in a tiny two-bedroom apartment. He enrolled at the Oliver Perry Middle School in the fifth grade. Usually, he was bulled by his new school mates. They would called him all sorts of names like *African Monkey*, *African Giraffe*, etc. whenever he told me, I would say something like, "You need to not let that get to you Max. Be strong or ignore it. Keep focusing on what you are here for, please." It always broke my heart.

One particular time, he didn't seem to take this advice, he asked, "But Ma, it is not fair. Why should I have to accept this? Perhaps if I did something, things would change."

I was partly embarrassed and ashamed to admit he was right but it felt powerless fighting a beast with wounded hands. Sadly, that was the way of America. I told him what I did, "I turn a deaf ear and a blind eye because I know what I am here for, so we shouldn't let any side attraction deter us from our aims."

Eventually, things turned around, the following year. He became president of his class and one of the most popular students in the school. I joined him in the United States of America on November 22 of that same year. Although we got an apartment in the Hartford Housing Project, the environment was not where we wanted to live. We, however, appreciated the kindness of the people around us. I had always taught my son that we should think big and dream big and that our expectations and imaginations should be on the things ahead of us that God has in store.

Maxwell's dreams were so much bigger than he was. As a child he would say what area he would live when he grew up, what his dream car would be and so much more. America to us opened up countless opportunities and possibilities. As a parent and a foreigner, it was my responsibility to walk into those challenges. So always, think big, the journey might be rocky and long. But some day, you will reach it.

As a mother, I always told my son, the proper way of life is respecting others and having an overall good reputation. This could carry a child a long way, in addition to going to school and learning books.

Our cousins, the Dunbars, lived in the housing project along with uncle Seh and his wife and another Liberian whose children were good friends of Maxwell. Most parents had two jobs in order to financially maintain our households and at the same time help our extended families back in Liberia.

Maxwell did not like where we were living, but I reminded him that I had promised to buy our own home one day before he graduated from high school.

Maxwell got enrolled in the Mt. Pleasant High School Managerial Science Programme; he became vice president during his Junior and Senior years and was also voted best dressed in the 11th and 12th grades in high school. He was also chosen who's Who among American high school students. He was later chosen as one of the candidates for a Brown University Programme, and was sent to a Brown University affiliated School in Mississippi because he had wished to become a Medical Doctor. This program was there to help minority students that wanted to become doctors.

Max seemed to be on the trajectory he had set for himself; one even I tend to like. Everything was falling into place. What could go wrong? Nothing; yet, everything seemingly did. Max had to leave the program and for what? A woman. Yeah, this is when you all think of the over protective, evil mother in law right.

But that was not entirely true. I guess mothers will always protect their children from any possible danger. Hardly anyone can spot danger more than a mother looking out for her children.

When his girlfriend, later wife, happened to have gotten pregnant with their first child, Amanda, he decided to marry her.

As a mother, wanting the fulfillment of his educational dreams, I was upset and did not speak to him for about three or four weeks. I could not see any other possibility but the track he had set for himself. He had worked so hard to be here. Now, he risked losing it all for a WOMAN! That didn't fly with me. It was not the girl per se but it was sure as heck personal. I felt that if she loved him, she would at least give him the chance to attain his dreams. They could have children later when he was done. I failed to see any other possibility. I was disappointed, frustrated and angry as hell. I felt karma was playing a crude joke on me. Was it something I had done way down the line? Or was life just swinging one of its shitty punches again?

Eventually, I gave in. Max was the one who showed me once more that nothing was beyond reach. He made me understand something I had suppressed so long, that it didn't 'exist'. In all my focus on a better life for him, I failed to consider that a woman was involved. This girl would be placed through something similar to what I had gone through and no woman deserved that. I had forgotten my pain and ignored the fact that my actions could send another child into the circle we had fought so hard to break. Was I selfish or self-preserving? It didn't matter to me once I realized what my actions could have possibly meant for the unborn baby and the mother. It wasn't easy before because I felt crushed but my experiences were too strong to cause another woman to go through anything resembling what I went through.

Max had promised that he would not put any woman through what I had gone through as a single parent. He was very true to his words. He got a job at B.J's Club, another at a nursing home as an aide and he drove a limo on the weekends to make ends meet. Maxwell and his wife moved upstairs from me, they decided to pay half of the mortgage, which was three hundred and fifty dollars a month and we all cooked and ate together.

Even at this time in his life, he was still setting career goals. He applied to the Department of Corrections to become a correctional guard and got accepted into it. He got his acceptance letter on a Friday afternoon but he had to present his medical papers on Monday when classes began. I knew the chief medical officer for the state of Rhode Island. I called him up and he set up an appointment for that Saturday at his Greenwich office and told us to be on time at 10: am to submit Max's specimen (urine). And then he began his career at the prison (the Adult Correctional Institute). He worked there for about five or six years and was also an auxiliary police with the Providence Police Department. Eventually, he applied when there was an opening within the system for employment, and was accepted. Thus began his police career.

As an African it is very important, we all eat from the same pots, this puts values on our African traditions and a society. This was also time for children to ask questions about the family and culture. It was a time where I could help to babysit their daughter to give them time that would allow them more quality time together as young couples.

I had just purchased our first home, a two family Colonial. It wasn't in the best of neighborhoods, but we were very proud of it. In December of 1989, the civil war broke out in our native country, Liberia. This was a very challenging period in our Liberian communities- socially, emotionally, and physically. We were all paralyzed from fear and this was taking a toll on my health. Culturally, I was raised to show compassion for less fortunate family members. Family members that were living abroad had to shoulder the burdens of their family members back home due to the civil war.

War Games; No Peace

Family, Death, Hardship

In January of 1990, I learned that my younger brother and other family members had been killed. The Charles Taylor's rebel faction had engulfed the entire country. The security issues worsened quickly when the rebel incursion began.

I had to raise ten to fifteen thousand dollars to purchase my plane ticket and also purchased tickets for some members of my immediate family. I worked extra shifts, took on a second job, cleaning houses and babysitting. I worked seven days a week.

Now I was faced with the fact of paying my montage, or having to travel to Freetown, Sierra Leone to look for my family. It was during that time, my co-workers at the Medical Center, where I worked as an aid, were supportive. Almost everyone made some kind of contribution like clothes collections or financial donations. People always called to encourage me.

Fear took hold of me; I had travelled from America to London, England, the gateway Airport to Freetown, Sierra Leone, Logai Airport. I sat on the plane waiting to disembark with the other passengers, my emotions started to play tricks on me - "will I be able to get off this plane, what am I doing here"? My only sense of purpose was God please give me the strength and courage to complete my journey, as you have brought me this far, please carry me through this.

Then I got off the ferry from Logai airport and got into a cab, the taxi driver was very nice, he assisted me by taking me to an inexpensive hotel, it was very clean and I paid about fifty US dollars that night.

Early the next morning my cabbie reported, to take me to the bus station for Kenema. I was able to get on the first bus out of Freetown for Kenema, and they told me that the ride could take about eight hours. We started our journey about 8am, around 11am our bus ran off the road, a minor accident; people had cuts and bruises. At this time I was in a panic mood. All kinds of thoughts ran through my mind, "Did I do the right thing by coming this far?" "Will we even reach safely?" I kept asking myself those questions because I had heard stories about how women were raped and even killed in these remote places. The delay meant we had to stay longer.

At that point, frustration was taking a hold on me because darkness was setting in, the sun was going down, and I am afraid of darkness. We finally arrived in Kenema around 7pm then my mind began to run wild with anxiety. I knew no one in this place. Then the least expected happened.

"Aunt Miatta!" someone shouted my name.

It took me a while to respond because I could not fathom who'd be calling me. My family call me sister Miatta or aunty Miatta. I took a few seconds to return his greetings. "Yeah," I feebly managed as I lifted my head. Standing right in front of the bus, as excited as anyone I have seen before was, Andramadi, my cousin. He walked up to me and hugged.

"Mama is right in the nearby village and your sisters and other relatives are living right in Kenema. But first, you have to buy me some food to eat because I have not eaten all day."

"Sure," I muttered as I realized that I too had not eaten all day. We went to a nearby cook shop and ordered. We took cassava leaf and rice - a Liberian dish. I could not eat the food. I sat there resisting the urge to squeeze answers out of him. I just could not, seeing how he devoured the food as if it was his first real meal in days. And truly, as I learned soon, it was actually his first in days.

"You are not eating?" He asked.

"No, I am not."

"Thank you," he said and with an urgency that only a starving person has, he grabbed my plate and happily gobbled mine quickly, and washed it with a bag and half of a mineral water.

Done and satisfied as a king, we hailed a taxi and went straight to my family's makeshift dwelling place. Hawa, my sister, Zinnah and Cousin Betty were all astonished to see me. They lifted up their voices and began to cry wallowing all about the devastation of the war.

I waited patiently until they all had calmed down; then asked about their wellbeing. Each one told me about the tragedy and other horrifying details of how the squad of rebel fighters had terrorized the entire community. My aunt Miatta, whom I was named after, had also been killed. Uncle JB and another older uncle that couldn't move from their houses were burned alive as rebels set their houses on fire. The stories went on and on until finally, they stopped in the middle of the night. I had already made arrangements with the cabbie the night before to pick us up and take us to Malamah near Bo

Waterside, another refugee camp where my mother and other family members were staying.

We left by 7:am that morning right after we had our baths. We made some stops along the way to buy bananas and some other tropical fruits to eat. Our ride was very rough because the dirt road was rocky and had water potholes along the way. The rainy season was coming to an end. A distance that should have taken us about three to four hours, took us eight and half hours.

When we arrived at our destination, my mother was sitting on the front porch of the little hut, again they were all surprised, she cried and cried and told me that I should not be there, the conditions were terrible. The hut that they had found in the refugee camp had been abandoned. My uncles Lincoln and Daffa had put palm thatches on the top for roof. The women had put mud to fix the floors and walls, whilst the windows were pieces of planks. It had no back door, only front door. It barely stopped the rain and sun.

My mother later told me that she had over thirty- two persons living with her in that unit. Just imagine how cramped it was, like a can of sardines. One room was for my mother and her grandchildren, while my uncle and his wife slept in the other room. There were people on the floor everywhere; every open available space was filled with refugees. After the greetings, I met some family members that I did not even know. Their little ones were so happy to see me; they were all over me playing with my hair, rubbing my arms and face, asking questions about America. I was not prepared for the difficulties especially the loss of my mother's son, sister and brother. It was such an emotional situation.

There were so many fatherless children and widows. All I could think about was who would defend the cause of these people, as most faced fear of the future and its insecurities. This was very crucial and I tried hard to hide my own emotions. I tried to empathize with them, but it was not possible. I had been through tough times in my life, real tough ones, but they felt pale compared to what I was seeing here. Perhaps it was because I had gotten out of mine and was now in a more comfortable place or perhaps, over time, distanced myself from the grief and pain. I don't know. I do know that I could not imagine going through what they had gone through.

The town chief of Malamah heard about my arrival and he came over. He asked, "My daughter, welcome. We do not have much but I could give you a place at my compound. They are more comfortable than here."

"Thank you chief. I appreciate it but please forgive me and allow me to be here with my mother and family. I can't afford to be distant from them, not now. I said that I rather sleep with my mother wherever she sleeps despite the conditions."

My mother and I spent the entire night discussing what I would be facing now that I was here. The next day I decided to do something good; after all, these were my very own relatives and compatriots. I know that I was unable to help the entire family, so I was going to have a little party.

Everybody decided to help with the little resource that s/he had. They began to bring rice by bags, coal, fish and oil that had been given to them by the United Nations. I bought two goats, few chickens, and some Soda pops from the villagers. We of course had good time. For the briefest of moments, they forgot about the war.

Around six to seven PM, rumors started circulating that Charles Taylor's rebels were attempting to enter into Sierra Leone by way of Bo Waterside, the next town to where we were. I begged my mother to leave the area, but she insisted that we wait until the next morning. However, before the day could break, the Taylor rebels entered Bo Waterside and all hell broke loose. We took a quick bath and left the area only with the clothes on our backs. Extra loads would not only slow one down but also place a crosshair on the carrier. Rebels could kill for things they wanted.

I along with other refugees started our walk from Bo Waterside. About 4am in the morning of March 28, 1991, my "menses" had just started with intense crimping and heavy bleeding. As we walked, the dawn turned into daybreak. By 7 to 8 am, the sun had come up scorching the Sierra Leonean skylines. We did not even hear or see the birds or any other animal. We walked and got thirstier by the minute but there was no water nor food. We just needed to live, the rest we could settle in time.

The journey was a long and difficult one. We walked until my feet hurt. Two women gave birth along the journey but could not carry on. The families had the difficult task of choosing to stay or go on. If they stayed, they risk certain death. If they went on, the mothers and or their children faced similar fate. In the end, the mothers, in both cases, gave the children up to families and remained behind.

With rebel forces hot on our heels, there was no time to even carry them. The blood loss and strain of delivery rendered them incapable of making the journey. Shortly after we left them, they were killed. Personally, this was the hardest point yet in the journey. I could not, for the love of life, imagine giving Max up just after delivery and simply waiting to die. I could not.

I soon realized that folks were more concerned about the greater group than individuals. If one risked being the cost of everyone dying, s/he chose to let more people live. These were not easy choices. No one feels good leaving a mother, father, grandparent or child behind to be killed. Sickness, handicap or other reasons were certain death. One had to be able to move at all cost. Failure to do so did not often end well.

As if we did not have more than enough problems, we had to deal with the many checkpoints. These makeshift roadblocks were tricky. Men, boys and sometimes girls, striped searched people every time. There was no privacy. We all stood there as prying hands went all over one's body. It was common to have fingers placed in one's private parts. The general explanation was that, people could hide ammunitions, valuables and other items there. Women were disrespected and degraded and no none thought better of it. Young girls were violated and even raped. Some were taken as wives for their bosses. This was an entirely different level of stress.

They were searching for things. YES, things. Anything of value. A wrong look, word, movement or response was enough to have one killed. That was our portion as women. The men, I think they got it worse. Many blamed them for the war and considered them facilitators in some way. They were often flogged, killed or flogged mercilessly then killed. The favorite forms were beheading, gutting mutilating or being shot in the back of the head.

Then some people were given a choice. They could select which method of death they wanted. If they were generous, they would ask the person to choose if s/he wanted sleeveless, short sleeves or long sleeves. A sleeveless cut meant amputation of the hand or leg from the shoulder or hip. Short sleeves meant from the elbow or the knee whilst long sleeves referred to amputation from the wrist or ankle. They let the person go after the deed. These amputations were crude. Most times, they used rustic blades, machetes or other instruments. They held victims down whilst another cut away. Many passed out and or didn't survive these operations.

At times, a person was asked to choose the method of death he or she preferred. In a time like that, you would need to trust the Lord. We kept one moving along the way, young children, men, women as well as older folks,

As hard as I tried to comprehend the situation, my mind just did not have the capacity to think or analyze it. However, as I looked around at the faces of the younger children, I was given hope and courage. Those moments spurred me on and defined every fiber of my being. I was never closer to my Lord.

When we reached our destination, we had no food, no water and no hopes of finding any. I asked people in the village for food to buy for the little children. Eventually, I was able to find farina/Gari (powered cassava tubal) that we bought for a hundred dollars a bucket. We also got some sugar.

I made the children sit in groups of six, ten, and twenty depending their sizes. As I glanced around, I gently walked within the crowd to see if there was more food available for me to purchase. The crowd

Miatta E. Dorley

was getting much larger than I anticipated.
I got peanuts, sweets with some drinking
water for the children to ete. After that,
some went right out to play. They just went
about being children for a brief while.

The challenges were just beginning; I
now had to deal with my transportation
issue. I needed to get out of Zimmi, but
there were no commercial cars plying the
routes. The only cars available were those
of some NGO's big trucks and they took on
board, only parents of very young children,
pregnant women, European and US
citizens. My US citizenship papers were in
process because I had just applied for it. I
admitted reluctantly to myself that I was
doomed to die there. I knew that only God
was able to get me out of there.

Meanwhile, my sisters Zinnah, Hawa
along with Betty, my cousin, were looking
for transportation to get me out of the area.
As God would have it, my uncle Seh heard
about my dilemma and decided to show up
to the rescue.

Going Home?

We drove about five hours from Zimmi into Kenema that night. I could not shake off the trauma of the past days. I needed to get out of Kenema, but could not because there was a four-hour layover for the next bus to Freetown. It arrived at 5:30am. I knew within myself that it would be only a matter weeks, if not days before the rebels would attack the area, and I refused to go through any more humiliations. I therefore decided that, family or not, I was leaving.

Some family members raised concerns about my safety based upon their own experiences. They warned me that the whole of Freetown had a curfew. This meant that people were being harassed. Anybody on the street at nightfall could be killed, kidnapped just anything could happen to the person. I, on the other hand, only longed to get out of that hostile environment. I had soon learned that the assumption that rebels would kill me if they knew I was from the U.S.A., was not accurate. Some people told me that if they learned that I am from America, they would let me go. I was warned not to confront or challenge any rebel because it would only make things harder for us all. The reality was that I was dodging bullets in a war zone and the rebels were out of control.

I kept on praying that God help me out of there. There were so many different rebel factions including the government forces, a relatively progressive group that was struggling to gain back control both in Sierra Leone and Liberia, etc. Each side sought to divide the countries even further apart.

Although, family members were determined to keep me in Kenema, my mind was focused on leaving early in the morning. Fortunately, I was the first person to purchase my ticket for Freetown. I boarded around 6am that morning and as we travelled along the countryside all I could see was the beautiful Sierra Leonean skyline, something that my anxious eyes missed and did not enjoy on my first trip. I was anxious but opted to get some relief.

As I relaxed in the front of the bus, I saw some villagers with pails of water on their heads, some women with babies on their backs, men moving about from one checkpoint to another. All I could do was grieve within because I knew that soon, most of those towns would be destroyed, and soon turned into ghost towns.

I reflected on my own childhood. I recalled what happened when the moon was out at nighttime, how we would play hide and seek, the echoes and sound of laughter. I pondered, "What has happened to those people in that part of West Africa? Have they all gone mad? Or is it the greed of the war Lords or the insensitivities of the government about the condition of her citizens?" The sound of the bus horn brought me back to this horrific reality, this form of injustice was being carried on, ultimately humans have been known to prey upon the weaker members of their society.

Although, it took me the entire day, I arrived in Freetown about 5:30pm. Some friends of my sister's took me around to find a hotel. However, the Bloomfield Hotel was the hotel of my choice; most Liberian refugees lodged there. It was jam packed with women, children, and few men.

As the kids played, I soon fell into trance. I did not see them; instead, I saw those starving, scared children I left behind. When I watched the adults laugh and joke, it reminded me how the family members I left behind were denied this simple pleasure in life. For the first time since coming to Africa, I silently wept. I poured out my soul and interceded for those that had to go through the horrors of the war.

I ordered some food, some sodas and tried to relax, but I could not shake off the feeling of guilt. A part of me wanted to be with them, another, wished to be as far away as possible.

My trance was broken by raised voices of the adults who had by now began arguing. I sat there quietly listening to people make comparison between the Liberian rebel factions and that of the Sierra Leonean counterparts. Right there, I knew that it was time to take my exit. I went into my room and had my first real night sleep in what seemed like forever.

The next morning I woke up to the sound of the birds singing near my window. I glanced at the clock on the wall, it was past 8am. I hurriedly took my bath, dressed and headed for my appointment to buy my ticket for Liberia. I met my Cousin Betty's friend, and Bendu along with some men, one of them called Varney. They took me to the airline office and I learned that it was the last flight to Monrovia; I told them that I would take my chances, I got my ticket, and we all left around 11:30am. With that done, we took a cab directly to a Liberian cook shop on Shaika Stevens Street. When we sat, I told everyone at our table to order for their food I would pay for it. I ordered some cassava leaves. I began to wonder why cassava leaves were eaten more regularly. I later learned that it was highly rich in iron and other minerals for the human body.

As we ate our food, we discussed my pending trip to Monrovia. Everybody had some kind of advice for me, which I took seriously because I had a little experience at the border where soldiers intimidated people.

I left the cook shop, with the others and walked around the city for a while and returned to the Bloomfield Hotel in anticipation of my trip. I sat chatting in the atrium until 8pm. I took an early bath, and had a sandwich and a cup of iced tea. I went right to bed and slept soundly until 7am the next morning. I hurriedly took a cup of tea and rushed to Hasting airport in Kissy by cab.

I boarded the aircraft quickly. The ride was a little bumpy as we descended into Monrovia, but otherwise smooth. We safely landed at the James Spriggs Field Airport in Sinkor, Monrovia, around 4pm. The entire city looked like a ghost town. There were little to no movements.

My heart began to ache and tears swallowed my eyes as I cried for my beloved country. There were burned cars all around, some with skeletons or bodies still inside. Dirt was all in the streets whilst entire neighborhoods were abandoned. A once beautiful city, laid in ruins. I was able to find a cab that took me to my house for $25; a distance that once cost ¢60. I was so grateful and I went right to my in-laws the Harris' in Mamba Point, no one was expecting me, so I introduced myself. My mother-in-law, a very sweet lady. She showed me so much love. We talked for a while, then she gave me a lappa to wear because I had no clothes to put on. I washed my clothes every evening and wore them the next day.

I really did not understand the devastation that the country had undergone. Tragedy was everywhere and being committed by people you least expected. I did not sleep that night, I was anxious. The sun still shone but the atmosphere had changed into hideous hopelessness. It was a terrifying place to live. Not even an animal could be seen in the streets of Monrovia. I mean not even a single bird was in sight as I walked around that morning. I would say pure desolation. I could not tell where I was going or what I was doing; I was a little afraid of leaving the house, but once again, I had to find the courage to take that bold step.

I strolled down Gurley Street where I lived in my late teens until I was twenty-one. I went to the house and gently placed knock on the front door. At first no one answered, I knocked a second and third time, than a small voice asked, "Who is it?"

"It is me Miatta."

"Miatta? I don't know any Miatta. The only one I know is in the USA, so you better say who you really are."

"It is me, Rojatu. I am here." Then she opened the door slightly and pulled me inside. We both broke down and cried, her younger daughter had just died from hunger and lack of medications. She was a registered nurse but could not save her child. Her second daughter (Nafisa) was suffering from malnourishment – swollen feet and hands, thinning hair, cramping stomach and just continuously crying. Imagine being a nurse and you are unable to help your own children.

I listened to my sister as she struggled to tell me tales of how the rebels had devalued her womanhood. The irony, she said as an R.N, she had been trained to save lives, and it disturbed her just to sit indoors with no help in sight. The rebels that came to protect us were the same ones harming, abusing and harassing us each day. As Rojatu spoke about the rebels, she noted that it was unsafe to be out in the streets because of our tribe, we were also a target (being half Mandingo).

Just as I was about to leave the room one of my brothers, Ansu, rushed into the hallway and vowed that his sister would not go out alone; not with all those rebel activities going on around, I tried my best to talk with him and another cousin was coming, but they refused my request.

I came outside with the others. We looked left and then right, we only saw the body of a man that had just been killed. It was too late to return or go back to where I came from because after we had walked just about four feet, a group of rebel fighters, mostly child soldiers, confronted us. As we began to talk to them about letting us go, I began to pray. We went on this back and forth for a while. My brothers would plead, the rebels would refuse and accuse us of something else. All this while, we were on our knees. My brothers had been striped to their undies.

Just when I could take no more, another group of rebels emerged from around the corner and argument broke out between both factions, one group said that they had the AK-47 rifles, while the other said they had the grenades. So they were threatening each other that they would use their weapons against one another. The argument went on for what seemed like an eternity. For some strange reasons, they allowed us to go. At that moment I knew that God had showered me with his grace; because the whole while I became invisible to their eyes; like they didn't even see me nor did they address me.

First of all, I had on a gold chain that was worth about six hundred dollars; a wrist watch that cost about one hundred and fifty United States dollars, and a pair of New Balance sneakers costing about sixty-five United States dollars. With all these, a person could easily get killed by the rebels. Their commanding officer had a ridiculous looking hair with red, white and green paint all over his face and body. He continued to argue about killing everyone in sight. My brother Ansu and my cousin were on their knees. They had sneakers and rags. After the argument, the rebels stripped them naked down to only their under clothes and then they told all of us to leave the area.

Untrained, irresponsible, and inhumane drug addicted armed men ruled over people. I saw child soldiers determine people's fates. If one had something they wanted, they took it. Little things like clothes, watches or jewelry, were potential death sentences to the owners. Fighters killed or maimed for it. It was jungle justice, only this time, the rebels dispensed it in any manner they saw fit.

I watched, girls being raped right before their parents or family members. I saw rebels rape women before their own husbands and no one dared to do anything.

Sporadic shooting was something to just always expect whenever you found yourself among those fighters. Firing could be a result of enemy attack or fighting amongst themselves for some looted items like vehicles, money, etc. (only the strong survived among them in a situation like that).

The war caused a complete breakdown of every fabric of our society- culturally, socially, economically, psychologically, politically etc. Culturally, we went bankrupt. For instance, children were no longer found obeying and submitting to the old folks of our society as it used to be before the war; the cultural values that were taught to the younger generation to be passed down to their successors were no longer working that way.

I arrived at my in-law's home around 8pm that night; my mother-in-law told me that they thought that I had gotten killed because she did not see me for the whole day. that's what happens around there. My sister Rojatu and I had arranged to get out of Liberia with an officer of the ECOMOG Peacekeeping force who arranged a space on a fighter aircraft. She was very fluent in Hausa, a language most of the troops from Nigeria spoke. For a small fee, my name was placed on the manifest and that was the only way I was able to get out of Liberia.

I arrived in Nigeria around 10pm. After going through Immigration and Custom, I asked for a hotel around Lagos, I slept in one close to the airport. I was exhausted from the trip and still had on the same clothes. I was fortunate that some of the soldiers that I met on the flight showed me around. I had nothing to check into the hotel, so I went down to the bar, ordered a glass of wine, and some food.

At that time, Liberian news was the hottest topic. Everybody was interested in hearing what was going on there. My order of food came in, I drank my last wine and left for my room, I hurriedly ate my chicken with rice, took a cold shower, and slept even more soundly for the first time in three weeks.

I woke up to the ringing of the phone. The same soldiers I had befriended on the plane had come to take me to the airport. I hurriedly showered and got dressed. We met in the hotel lobby, talked briefly and went out to their car. That is the Africa I remembered, one where a stranger helps you without even knowing anything about you. We drove to the airport and I could not believe my eyes. Wow, Lagos was so beautiful and captivating. I could not get a flight out of Lagos for two days. I went to shop for some clothes and I moved into the

Federal Place Hotel on Victoria Island, I turned my stay into mini- vacation, and at last it was time for me to board my flight for New York City.

As I journeyed from Lagos to New York, I began internalizing the events. I had a different understanding. It was unfair to criticize family member for not wanting to do anything, as some overseas did. I kept playing the scene over and again. The things that I had seen both in Liberia and in Sierra Leone solidified the reality that war is not good. The insanity that comes with it as people's lives are overturned were enough to humble anyone.

Seeing how the infrastructure was broken, no electricity, no running water, the sewage system was down, food had to be rationed and dumps of garbage all over the country. The city was infected with flies and cockroaches and rats were everywhere.

No flight in and out of the country. I could not get it out of my mind. People all around were so miserable; the only news outside of Liberia was what was reported on CNN or BBC. I came out of my daydreaming when the pilot announced that we should fasten our seat belts for landing, I adjusted my seat, put my tray away as the plane landed along the run way and came to a halt.

Back in America

Family, Life, Healing

I got out with other passengers at the New York JFK airport. Once again, I came across people anxiously waiting for friends and loved ones as I went to get a connecting flight for Rhode Island. I arrived home exhausted from a very long journey; I gave my family lengthy accounts of what was happening in Liberia and Sierra Leone. One phase of the journey was over, now I focused on how to get my family out of the war zone.

I got my American citizenship after my return to the United States. Filing my mother and stepfather's papers was an easy process but my life was never the same, I would have nightmares about the war. Eventually, I learned of a program by Representative Joseph Newsome called the Rhode Island, Liberian initiative. I was able to get involved and bring my nieces Small Miatta Gul and her brother Emmanuel Gul between 1992 and 1993, I was able to bring along my mother and Stepfather. But my sisters and other relatives I couldn't get over.

After the arrival of the children, there seemed to be many more challenges that awaited me: Maxwell had been the only child living here all along, now he was forced to share my attention with some children that he did not know. His daughter Amanda was a toddler and I did most of her babysitting while her parents went to school and worked.

At that time, we were living on 14 Benedict Street. Max, his wife Kou and their daughter lived upstairs from me. Emmanuel, Miatta and I lived downstairs. Small Miatta had to be bussed to the south side of

Providence to attend Martin Luther King Elementary School, while small Bobby aka Emmanuel went to school on the west end, at Gilbert Stout Elementary School.

Starting all over again with two children was very hectic. Doing the rounds, putting kids on the bus for school, making lunches, washing and preparing clothes for school or church etc., was a handful. But most of all, what I enjoyed was the different personalities.

One day, whilst sitting watching TV, Amanda came in and told small Bobby, "Do not sit near grandma Miatta. She is my own self grandma."

Lost for words, Bobby and the rest of us burst into laughter. The fights were many-in the car and out, just about any place if the conditions were right. It was not all fight, it was different and just something I hardly experienced with Max.

However, I soon got a hang of it in general. Young Amanda grew from wanting me to send Bobby and his family back to Africa to accepting them as the family they were. T hose were moments that I will always cherish.

These children were the only thing left from my brother that I could hold on to. God had helped me to bring them abroad into a new life, new environment and new country. Looking back now, I've come to realize that the choices I have made affected my entire family. Loved ones as well as my own life was changed forever. From this perspective I wouldn't have changed anything or done it differently, to some extent, we do have control over some parts of our own destiny.

Back in 1992 after the arrival of Miatta and small Bobby, I was diagnosed with rheumatism and thyroid disease, a month into their staying in America I came down with heavy bleeding and I got severely ill and had to be hospitalized. I had surgery that put me into semi-coma for few days at the Providence Women and Infant Hospital under the care of Dr. D'Orio. After recuperating from the hospital, I began to experience strange dreams about things before they even happened. For instance, before the 911 attack on New York, I dreamt that there was a disaster. In my dream, there appeared to have pieces of human body parts everywhere and I prayed that God would intervene to save the nation. And then I was instructed to pray for the nation particularly to pray for president George W. Bush as a prayer assignment. As I prayed for him so personally, it made my prayer team members wonder if I knew him personally and I told them no, it was just an instruction from the Lord.

Another instance is the Katarina disaster and flooding in New Orleans and an earthquake that were in my dream. I told my prayer team and we began praying. When the earthquake took, the effect was minimum or had lesser effect on the state of Rhode Island. Sometimes I will just come out with certain information.

After I got out of the hospital, things got very bad with me financially and health wise. I could not even afford gas to heat up my home that winter. I had major health issues and lost my balance in walking. The doctor told me that I would not be able to walk again. The old car that I had, broke down and things just got worse. One day, I just locked myself indoors and prayed endlessly to God, I cried and told him that he did not allow me to bring these little children that had no father, and then I did not know if their mothers were alive.

In my deep distress, I pleaded and surrendered myself to God's will. Within a month's time, I had a major breakthrough. I had been out of job. Because of worker's compensation before Surgery, I was able to get back pay, and things begin to come alive again. At that time Max's, his wife Kou, and their baby daughter Amanda, had moved to a new neighborhood and apartment. The kids and I lived on 14 Benedict Street until March of 1993 and then we moved to 25th Armington Avenue. I returned to work and in a few years, I bought another home. This time, it was on 25th Melissa Street in the city of Providence, RI. Things went good for a while until the turbulent teenage years.

I remarried only to find myself in hell all over. Life got complicated partly because of the additional children that my new husband had brought into the marriage. In the end, the marriage did not last. My health continued to decline until 2008 when my doctor decided to place me on permanent disability. I later sold my house that was on Melissa Street and moved in with Max and his family on 4th Falcon Crest Dr. in the city of Johnston RI until I went to visit a friend Betty in Redding PA. While there one night, I had a dream that my son Max was involved in an accident and he got killed around 2:am that morning. I woke and called Max. I told him about my dream, he was so upset, and I could do was tell him to pray about it. I had a dream before about him being involved in car accident but never about him dying in it.

I just continued praying for him, I even called up my aunty in-law who is a pastor and some other pastors, friends and even my prayer team that also joined in my prayers for Max. I had prior dreams about minor accidents and the lord kept telling me to tell him to leave the job or else he would get killed on the job. There are certain things about people that are intimately close to me that I wouldn't just want to know.

There are prophetic signs at times that one would not like to know about himself or herself or a close relative. But something strange began to happen to me: I started to have all of these things happening, sometimes in my dreams, and sometimes I would just know about them but I would feel reluctant to ask. One day I just came right out and asked him about his job as if he was having some issues there, and he told me yes. But that he was afraid to tell me because he did not want me to start worrying. I just told him that I was his mother and it was my duty to worry about things that happen to him. Max explained in details about some of the problems that he was encountering while working at Providence PD.

One example was, one of his fellow Police officers had asked to borrow some cash but Max had to meet him at Lincoln's woods Casino. He Max called me up and asked what he should do. I had an uneasy feeling about the whole situation, I told him not to do it. If he really wanted to borrow the cash, he should do it at the station in the presence of witnesses.

Two or three weeks later, the guy was arrested and put in jail. The department had gotten a new police chief and this guy did not like minority officers at all and he was causing a lot of problems to the point that he wanted to leave the Providence PD. He started experiencing anxieties to the point of panic attacks. He felt that people were following him. As his mother, I talked him into counseling and I kept praying for him.

Max was put on paid leave in 2010. He used this opportunity to visit his native homeland Liberia for the first time. Before coming, he asked many of his co-officers to donate their used uniforms. He then donated those uniforms to the Liberian National Police. The country was still suffering from the devastation of 14 years of civil war. This gesture made national news headlines; many people in and out of Liberia were so impressed with this act of his.

Although he had his own issues, he was able to help a few of the country's orphans pay their school fees, buy books and school uniforms. Max returned with a different mindset. He was to return to college and finish his studies. He'd work for the Providence PD for five more years and then retire. At the time, he had moved his family to the state of Georgia.

In 2011, I received this urge from the lord one day while praying that I should pray for Max's salvation. I prayed with a prayer partner from Bethel Church at St. Paul

Bridge in Liberia by phone whom my nephew connected me with.

I continued to pray until July of 2011 on Wednesday, after I was done praying, I heard the Lord again that Max's was all right that he had received his salvation. Meanwhile, Max had resumed his duty at the police station, but was on desk duty in the record room and a lot of the women there were saved. Our Lord has a way of dealing with situations his own way. He could call me up for scriptures and ask bible questions. We talked daily as mother and son. There is a faithful saying, "all the ways of the Lord are loving and faithful towards those who keep the demands of his covenant" (Ps) 25:10.

Max has started on a spiritual journey and only God's grace had led him on that path. In November of 2011 I decided to move back to Liberia, because of serious health issues. I discussed it with my family and we all agreed. I came into Providence, Rhode Island to spend some time with Max and turned him over to my sister Hawa because it was our custom to always leave family members in the hands of the next oldest in line. That was the last time that I had seen my child alive. I arrived in Liberia mid-November of 2011 after three weeks with aid of some friends back in the US I decided to host a Christmas party for my neighborhood children. That was very successful and it was organized with the help of the people in my community Thinker's Village. The children were very happy for their Christmas.

I started a small prayer group right within my home, we met every Tuesday to pray for nations around the world and that during that time the Lord began to show me things in my dream. One night, I had a dream that something happened to him at the police station. I saw things I was uncomfortable with; I could not even think about them.

I tried my very best to get in touch with Max but it was not happening. I also asked my sister Hawa to tell him that I needed to speak with him because I didn't want to tell anyone about what I had seen in the dream but the call would not go through. That went on for almost a month. When we talked, I would just forget to talk about the dream or the call would not just go through.

However, I became so restless, I just could not put my fingers on this uneasy feeling that I was having, I could not sleep at night, I could not keep any food down but I just blamed it on the surgery that I had some time in March of 2009. All I could say was Roman 8:28 tells me that all things work together for those that love God, and are call according to his purpose. As believers we continue to gather to pray for the nations. On 18 April 2012, I received a call from Max telling me that he had sent me some money to help me with the church building that was being constructed in our village. This was around 10:30pm, I had gone to bed.

He told me that he sent the money by Money Gram. I thanked him for everything. I knew that he had to work a lot of details just to help me out. Max called me again the second time around 1:30 am on Thursday morning Liberia's time, just to make sure I had heard him and to make sure that everything was all right because I sounded a little upset. He said as believers, we should always let things go. We concluded our talk.

On the 17th of April 2012, just after our prayer meeting ended and I was about to serve some snacks for lunch to the group, I step into my room, I heard a voice said to me go back out there and tell the group to start praying for you because of the challenge that you are about to face. I finally went out and explained to the group my encounter with the Lord in my bedroom. I could not overcome these uncertain feelings I was having. I sat down to prayed; then my sister in-law Josephine placed a knocked on the door and came in, we both sat down and sipped some lemonade. When my glass slipped and scattered, Josephine and I looked at each other without saying a word-telepathy. We both knew that this was an omen in our culture signifying a bad sign.

According to our tradition, there are couple of things that whenever they happen to a person, it means either a good or a bad sign. For example, the trembling of an eye, the stumbling of the left foot, an abrupt falling to the ground, digging of soil or cassava in one's sleep and many others are all negative or bad signs. I cleaned up in total silence and went to bed about 1 to 3am that morning. I had a dream where I saw two closed caskets; one with a certain cream color clothes with a maroon cross in the center of it. And in my dream, everything that had to do with the person, in it belonged to me and that I had to make some decisions. I had seen all of my old friends in a huge hall, all of them dressed up in black, I recognize some faces and some I did not.

But the strangest thing that happened to me in the dream was that, I opened the other casket, but did not know the person and he was younger then my son. I woke from that nightmare in heavy sweat and my whole body was shaking. I prayed about the dream and the answer that I received was a premature death of a loved one. I ran down the hall and knocked on my mother's door to tell her about my dream and after I told her, she just looked at me and said nothing.

Prior to that night back in February and March, I had gone to town to change my flight to come back to the States. But every time I reached the sales associates desk, I always changed my mind. It happened about three times. Later, I made new plans to travel on the twenty 25th of April 2012. I woke up that early morning of April 19 with a serious heaviness. Then I got ready for town because

I was leaving very soon. I went to town collected the money that Max had sent by Money Gram, I called Pastor Nelly to come and pick up the money for the newly constructed church. I had already spoken to her about things that the newly constructed church needed, and all went well. I then told the driver that he needed to get the car ready like God was just directing me along the way.

For example, I did not realize that all of the clothes I had bought were all black and white; my suitcase had been packed for about three weeks. I did everything and got back home around 2:30pm and I noticed that people from my prayer group had arrived at my home. I asked what it was all about, and they told me that they were just visiting. They realized that I did not know about Max's death. I still could not put together what was happening. Other friends that were in Liberia visiting all came to my home. It was swarmed with cars but I still didn't know what was happening. Just as I was about to settle, my mother's phone rang. She always had it on speaker. I heard Hawa on the other end asking for me, and if there was any male family around to give me the news. Right there I took the phone from my mother and asked her what happened to my son? She told me that there had been an accident.

And Max was in the hospital, I told Hawa that I knew that Max was dead because of the awful feeling I had within my stomach, suddenly my yard was fully crowded. All I could do was to sing this song, I must tell Jesus, I must tell Jesus, Jesus alone can carry me through. I went into my room and said a prayer and asked the Lord for his strength. And with the help of God, and VP of Liberia at the time, Joseph Boakai and I were able to rearrange my flight for the 20th of April 2012. I quietly boarded my flight to the United States for my son's funeral. That was the longest and most difficult flight I had ever taken in my entire life. At times I would seem as if I am about to faint until I arrived in Rhode Island.

Around 11:30pm on Saturday night Max's friend from the Providence Road, Jessy and my adopted son, small Bobby, were at the airport to pick me up. On seeing them, I was filled with emotion. It hit me that really Max was dead! After we all got into

Jessy's car and drove in total silence (a 40 minute drive from the airport) we arrived at my destination G. Katherine. Dr. Johnston with a large group of police officers and people from the Liberian community waiting on hand to meet me. I broke down and wept, as I gathered bits and pieces of the accounts of Max's death, the Lord put a song into my heart –In Your Presence, I Found Healing.

The rest of that week, I went about in a daze as the family went about getting ready for Max's funeral, life seemed to have gone from my body. Although I was aware that yes Max was dead physically, yet my mind refused to accept it and we were still communicating only that he had travelled to a distant country. I tried to think but I could not think, I just kept saying NO to myself, and if this were true, it was only a nightmare. My "reality base "was very limited at that time; I kept putting on a strong and brave face as I watched that whole scene being played out in a movie. I continue to struggle during those moments. I learned to depend on God totally. Why? Because it was the only hope that had given me solace.

Every so often, I could weep and crawl on the floor even though cops and other friends were around, everyone around me was invisible at those moments; my heart was pounding louder and louder. I felt faint at the realization that my child was really dead. I wept day in and day out. The Providence Police Department took control of the funeral arrangements. As family, we only gave them some details of what we wanted. My friends stepped right in and took me shopping to get out first and for some quiet time. The funeral parlor was on our way, my girlfriend Laurine asked if I wanted to make a stop at the morgue to see his body, but I refused because I did not want to see him before the wake or funeral.

We therefore waited onto the Garden City Mall in Cranston in total silence. The ice was broken when one of the sales associate said to my friend Laurine that they were asking customers to park their cars in a particular area because of the death of the Providence Police Officer. She then explained to the associate that the officer's mother was in the store that day, they all came up to me and gave their condolence.

We did our shopping and went on our way. My friends along with the people of Rhode Island showed me and my family along as well as the Providence Police department gave me tremendous amount of support during our time of bereavement. And I am just so grateful to them.

Providence Mayor Angel Travers and Providence Police Chief Hugh Clements along with his entire department were present almost every day. My greatest surprise came at the wake when I looked out at the car window and saw that there was a Police Car Stationed at every intersection.

My son Max was given so much honor during his wake keeping and funeral. But even before the funeral, I volunteered to help my sister Hawa and my daughter-in-law's mother to do the food preparation , it was the last thing that I could do by receiving his friends from the Providence PD. Call lines were long for hours without end. Max was given full police honors in Sneedville Georgia, on May 2nd of 2012 due to him leaving, his family relocated in Loganville Georgia, where he had planned living during his retirement years.

And again Col. Clement and most of Max's friends were on hand to see him at his final resting. No matter how strong a mother may be, the death of a child is so devastating that it destroys you to a coil. I became very irrational with some of my decision making as they were very personal. At this time, I began to criticize myself for not being around to see him before his death. I did the blaming game, Cece Winnas and Nicole Muller became my basic sources of inspiration in my praying state of mind. With their songs like "My Redeemer Lives, I am, call on Jesus and Alabaster Box." I would play these songs for hours; I could not even sleep, but just walk for days with no end. I even asked God for death, but death would not come.

The pain in my heart was so severe. I sometimes felt that Jesus had left me all along, but when I look back now, I realized that it was during those lonely and darkest days that my lord, carrying me along the way, Cece Winnas throne soon was my music of choice. I asked Jesus daily that I should not walk this walk alone. Tragedy in my life did not define my true character, but it did give meaning for my strength and weakness. No matter what the situation is, at that moment I just knew that I could rise above my circumstances. The loss of a child causes so much pain, discouragement, the anger, the mood swings. This is one trauma that I would not wish on my most hated enemy. Isaiah 43:2 and 3, I knew one of the ways that I could find some kind of serenity was to take a journey to Israel, that I did in November 2012-December 4, 2012.

This was a spiritual journey I was re-baptized in the Jordan River, I needed God's guidance and help, I had purposed in my heart that I would not be a vulnerable victim, I knew the power of God, with the help of my sister Hawa and friend Helena to lean on and I was good to go.

My very existence was on survival. To get out of bed each morning, I had to call on Jesus and ask him to restore my strength. Max's death had paralyzed and broken me to the coil. I had forgotten how to do the basic things that I did before. I could not remember how to do them; everybody just assumed that I was so strong. But the fact was that my sister Hawa was my pillar of strength. Every day she reminded me to be strong or else I would be put into the mental hospital. At this time my doctor had put me on some medication because I could not sleep for days or even weeks. I would stay up all night and broke down. One day, things had gotten so bad that Hawa had to call some friends from Liberia to a prayer vigil. They came and prayed with me. During this time, the Lord give me an idea, during the time of Max's funeral, his friends at Providence Police Department sold T-shirts in his honor. I decided to do the same by printing some T-shirts and calendar to sell them for some of the issues that he stood for.

I remember back when Max was a child, he would gather his friends and ask that I please give them some food to eat because they were hungry. Another instance of his generosity was the day before he travelled to the United States, he told me who I should give his clothes that he was leaving behind to. I am trying to show the kind of person he really was through the eyes of his mother.

Take for, example the homeless and the family that lived in a housing development. During his lifetime, Max and some of the police officers would donate toys and kids clothes to these families. I however decided to continue his legacy in whichever way I could; if for nothing but to keep him alive. Although I was very sensitive, most of the things that I did would not have made any sense to me today. I guess to keep the peace, my sister Hawa went along with whatever I wanted. Hawa and I went from to door to door selling T-shirts and calendars. I took buses and went out to distant States selling. I remembered during one of those trips in Camden, New Jersey my girlfriend

Helena was taking me to sell some of those calendars and a female police officer stopped the car. I just broke down and could not stop crying. The cop explained that she noticed our vehicle go around in circles and if she could be of any help. Helena and the other woman in the car told her that I had just lost my son and he was a Providence Police Officer, she gave me her condolence.

Grieving Badly

Losing Max took me to a dark place- a very dark one. I was angry, even bitter at times. I expected everyone to grieve as I did.

Feel as much as I felt; weep as much as I did etc. anything short of that was unacceptable. I failed to, was unable to see outside of my hurt; beyond my pain.

One of my saddest and difficult moments was during cops' week in DC May of 2013, when Max's kids really did not have anything to do with me. I was so fragmented and bruised from within; yet I longed to embrace Maxi's two children, Amanda and Robert.

However, before leaving for Washington DC, I apologized for any wrong or hurt I had caused them.

The fact is that, I had just lost my whole family, Max's wife and children had gone astray from me because of some family feud. So I was dealing with all of these emotional issues. I just did not care any more about things or anybody; the kids refused to call or even speak with me during this period.

In this state, I made some mistakes. In fact, too many mistakes where it counted the most, with my family. I had inadvertently pushed Max's wife away. I never stopped to consider her, at least not seriously. I failed to understand that she was also aggrieved. In some ways, I shamefully must admit, I blamed her for not grieving as much, hard and intensely as I did. Max was my son, my boy, if she did not wish to mourn for him, then I would do it.

In her own way, she was mourning. She was going through something I did not understand because I allowed myself to be blinded. I now know that she had it rough. I thought I did then, but I did not. Her decision to stay away from me and keep the kids was not unfounded. She needed to, if for no other reason than to protect the kids from this darkness.

This wasn't my finest hour, not at all. But thank God we overcame this phase in our lives. We now have a relationship that I believe is better. We moved beyond and closer than ever. In fact, in many ways, she has warmed my heart. She is now even more my daughter than an in-law. Perhaps, if this had not happened, we might not have appreciated each other as much as we do now.

I believe, a child is a gift from God, when I lost that gift, it seemed like my life was over. From where could I pick up the pieces? The only strength was being in the presence of God; no amount of therapy could heal me, my spirit has been broken, my joy had left my face, my life seemed like it was all over, a vacuum had been created in my heart. But in my moment of sorrow I learned to dwell in the secret place of the most high.

Reflecting

Today, many things make more sense. Some still I have to struggle with- here and there. I wish I could say the pain is gone. I wish I could say that the hole in my heart is filled. Unfortunately, it is not.

However, I am no longer at that low, dark place I used to be. In fact, I am at peace with aspects of my life and that should count for something. It certainly does.

I am happier than I was after Max died. I am more confident than I was. I am more optimistic than I was. I have found more reasons to live and carry on Max's legacy.

I have closed few chapters of my life and opened up new ones. I see a light often, and when I can't, I allow myself to breakdown then get up again.

About the Author

Miatta E. Dorley is of Liberian heritage. Her life is a testament to her resilience.

Since Max's death, she has relocated to Liberia where she runs the Sgt. Maxwell R. Dorley Foundation, which does feeding programs and medical outreach for less fortunate children in Liberia. The foundation hopes to extend its services to Sierra Leone and other parts of the world.

With the House of Hope Ministry, she continues to spread the Word and exercise her faith.

Made in the USA
Middletown, DE
17 May 2019